PRASE FOR SHIRLEY G

"There is throughout…that certainty: no other word, no form would express that thought, that feeling. (Lim) edges ahead of her rivals by the sheer confidence of her verse."

—Martyn Goff
Chief Executive, Book Trust
awarding the Commonwealth Poetry Prize for
Crossing the Peninsula

"The poet is in exile, but a counter-exile that permits an embracing of all contradictions."

—*World Literature Today*

"(Lim's) poems probe a woman's many and changing truths in language that will deepen the vision of every reader."

—Alicia Ostriker
author of 16 poetry collections, winner of the Patterson Poetry Award, the San Francisco State Poetry Center Award, and William Carlos Williams Award, and author of numerous critical studies

"In lifelong exile, Shirley Geok-lin Lim writes new poems from countries and islands all over the world. Her awed voice reaches our ears, and we get to know ourselves from myriad views."

—Maxine Hong Kingston
winner of the National Medal of Arts, numerous national book awards, and author of ten books, including *The Woman Warrior*, *China Men*, and *Tripmaster Monkey*

"Shirley Lim searches for hope and home as she moves around the globe…. she evokes and makes palpable a peace in the natural world's demands, resilience and beauty."

—Florence Howe
  Founding Director and Publisher of the Feminist Press,
  author of *A Life in Motion*, editor of *No more masks!* and
  numerous other collections

"[W]ith passion for exact observation, Shirley Geok-lin Lim writes of nature's grandeur, of social injustice and solidarity, of release from compulsion in a personal epic of universal woes and ways…Here we have…a gifted human's striving, treasuring, and hard won triumphs, a great poet's unstinting self-revelation."

—Barry Spacks
  author of *Food for the Journey* and nine other volumes of
  poetry

"Shirley Lim's poetry simultaneously puzzles and clarifies. These poems are rich in sense of place and startling juxtapositions… . They move and surprise like the cracks and slides of the earth."

—Diane Thiel
  author of ten books of poetry, non-fiction and pedagogy

IN PRAISE OF
LIMES

Poems by

Shirley Geok-lin Lim

SUNGOLD EDITIONS • SANTA BARBARA
2022

www.shirleygeoklinlim.com

Published by Sungold Editions

Cover by Gwen Frankfeldt
Author photo © 2021 Mia Nie

ISBN-13: 978-0-9991678-7-8

For my sisters,
Shelley Fisher Fishkin
and
Nina Morgan

CONTENTS

PREFACE

IN PRAISE OF LIM

By Dana Gioia

I first met Shirley Geok-lin Lim forty years ago in Katonah, New York. It was an unlikely encounter. I was from Los Angeles. She was from Malaysia. Both of us were unknown and unpublished poets living in Westchester County. We had come to a poetry reading at the Katonah Public Library to hear the late William Jay Smith. I don't remember how we actually met. We were probably introduced by Robert Phillips, who organized the reading. He had a genius for putting people together.

I do recall our awkward first conversation. Shirley was very shy, indeed laconic. That seems impossible, knowing her today, but I swear it was so. She had recently started teaching at Westchester Community College. We were both displaced young poets, adrift in suburbia, eager to connect with our own kind. But we couldn't seem to find a connection.

Finally, I asked a polite but banal question about her graduate studies in English. Shirley replied that she had worked at Brandeis with J. V. Cunningham. His was not a name to impress most people, but to me, Cunningham was a gold standard. He was the greatest American epigrammatic poet—ever. He was also a formidable scholar, mordant curmudgeon, and semi-recluse. *Tell me more*, I said. And she did.

A year later Shirley sent me her first book, *Crossing the Peninsula & Other Poems* (1980). Published in Kuala Lumpur by Heinemann Asia in a tiny format, the book gave the impression of slightness. I always worry when reading a book of poems by an acquaintance, Will I like it? Will it be interesting or awful? In Shirley's case, I was immediately engaged, though I recognized her debut volume was a very unusual collection.

Most first books have a grab bag quality. Young poets want to show all their steps toward creative maturity—different styles, subjects, and stances. Lim's book did that, too, but with an unusual economy and panache. The poems had ambitious subjects—Adam and Eve, Christ, shopping, divorce, Cezanne—but they were mostly short. They didn't waste a word. (Surely the terse Prof. Cunningham's influence at work.) Few young poets show such control, especially mixed with such an appetite for ideas and experience.

I was raised in an extended immigrant family, so I've always been alert to the complexities of people shaping their identities in a new country. Some want to preserve their old lives on new soil. Others open themselves to transformation in the new society. Lim is the poet laureate of the second group. She has an omnivorous imagination eager to devour ideas and experience in the new culture. Paradoxically, she is also the peripatetic elegist of the first group—exploring Asia in search of her complicated past.

At the end of her first volume is a short poem, "To Li-Po." For me, the poem served as a key to much of her work. It shows Lim reading the classic Tang Dynasty poet as a sort of foreigner. Her mixed ancestry of native-born Malayan with a Chinese grandfather allows her to feel a connection to the master poet, but she must approach him as an outsider to his language and culture. There is no single identity for Lim to discover and adopt. She must create a new person capacious enough to fit her international origins and adulthood. In America the complexity of her identity is doubly complicated--first by immigration and then by marriage and motherhood. As a poet, Lim doesn't take much from Walt Whitman, but she does fulfill one of his great bardic boasts—she is large, she contains multitudes.

I soon added "To Li-Po" to a new edition of *An Introduction to Poetry*, which I co-edited with X. J. Kennedy. Since then I have hardly published an anthology which did not include one or more of her poems. It gave me pleasure to share her work, especially "Learning to Love America," which has gradually become an anthology standard. It has also become a favorite poem to memorize and perform among high school students in Poetry Out Loud.

It may seem from my account that Shirley and I were the chummiest of friends. The truth is that I hardly knew her except through her poems. We met face to face in New York only two or three times. After those early sightings, I lost touch with her for twenty years. The books, however, continued to arrive at unpredictable intervals and published in an exotic sequence of places—New South Wales, Singapore, Hong Kong, London or Albuquerque. (My bibliography seemed provincial in comparison.) I had no idea where Shirley was or what she was doing, but it was clear she had gone global. I followed her profuse creativity on the page. The charm, humanity, and freshness of her poems never ceased to captivate me. As my admiration steadily grew, I was puzzled why she remained so little known in poetry circles.

Twenty years later we met at another poetry reading, this one my own at University of California, Santa Barbara. It took me a moment to recognize her. She was, I discovered, a professor there, indeed a very celebrated professor, but not in poetry. Shirley was now a major voice in Asian-American Feminist Studies. At last, the situation was clear. Like Hollywood, academia believes in typecasting. In the specialist world of the university, you can only be known for one thing. Shirley was a celebrated cultural studies theorist. Her poetry, as the theorists say, had been marginalized.

I can offer no opinion on Professor Lim's academic work, but I feel confident in declaring her poetry a rare achievement. In book after book, she has created a more impressive oeuvre than many writers who have professorships in poetry. Another U.C. Santa Barbara professor (long before Shirley's time), the brilliant Hugh Kenner once described American Modernist innovation as a "homemade world"—unorthodox creativity free from pomp, precedent, and pretension. Shirley's best poetry has that "homemade" quality. Like Wallace Stevens, she has put a planet on the table, a "homemade world" of her own experience.

Lim is a poet of exile and assimilation, loss and recovery, journeys and explorations. To her own astonishment, she has finally become a poet of arrival and abidance with Santa Barbara as her Ithaca. In each of her last few books, she has struggled with her relationship to the mythic Golden State and its quotidian reality. In "Learning to Love America," she pokes, she mocks, she tastes, and she ultimately embraces her new home because—in a poem made up of "because" clauses—it is now the reality of her complicated life.

> because to have a son is to have a country
>
> because my son will bury me here
>
> because countries are in our blood and we bleed them
>
> because it is late and too late to change my mind
>
> because it is time

In Praise of Limes is the culmination of her imaginative odyssey. She praises, rebukes, teases, and caresses her adopted California, a land of fruit and fire, a paradise perpetually in the process of being lost. *In Praise of Limes* is a book rhapsodic and elegiac by turns. Lim is caught between hope and anxiety but never remote from the bliss of being alive:

> I've forgotten how not to hope. We throw open
>
> the windows, draw water we do not have,
>
> as if wishes are promises are heaven
>
> on earth, and here and now forever safe.

Dana Gioia is the former Poet Laureate of California. His most recent collection is *99 Poems: New & Selected*, which won the Poets' Prize.

PASSING THROUGH

Passing Through

The mountains are brown, close enough
to see dry ridges and scarred trails.
Ocean's a reflection in the sky.
Winter rain promises in little puffs,
gray, silver-tint, then gone to sunny glow.
Santa Barbara, Santa Ynez,
Santa Claus: saints of history
flash past by south to San Diego.
If poetry is imitation, California
is a poem, easy on the eye, bright as
a new quarter, richer than a
hundred and twenty states, larger
than fifty countries. We swallow blue
Pacific, Amtrak and Greyhound, gold
dust and star dust, sixteen wheels
and twenty-ton trailers passing through.

Santa Barbara Rain

Morning after the rains, blossoms
pop up yellow among their weedy
tendrils; white in the citrus massy
branches; scarlet burning bush plums

budding; purple in the sage;
and orange, orange, orange poppies
to say, *Hello, California.* These,
like poems common on the page,

lowly or showy, tall sprung spiky
splurges out of succulents
that survive on dew, sky silent
sprinkled as, surprised by rain, we

forget our dry winter heat. Poetry
needs rain in drought years like creeks
need rain to murmur, like dried sticks
need rain to root, and roots to be

the trees written in their memory,
like angels need rain to praise
heaven, like babies need rain to raise
their sippy cups, like the poppy

needs rain to wave on its stem,
like I need rain to write the poem.

New Year's Eve

Becalmed, the mild air deceives. Each leaf
rests as if tranced on the pillowed hour.
The black cat sees me saunter streets away,
bounds like a hound, mole-scent pause broken.
Above, squadron on squadron, crows move
more sociable than families whose
night's squabbles still din in sleep, echoing
the squawks outside locked doors.
                                    Chinese Christmas
icicles shoot through pepper trees. Plywood
candy canes, pink-striped, dangle by garage eaves.

American appetite feeds engorged vision,
sleeps off binges this Sunday dawn, cars home
new-sleek for the year or battered, given
their screeching flight for the hour to crows.

Persephone

Early spring invisible spirits twitter
among the wet leaves. A boy pedals
his little bicycle, a loud chatterer
by his father as they speed toward school
the first daylight savings time Monday.
A mad man mouths into a microphone,
and Earth shudders, Persephone unable
to escape his white-knuckled grip on day.
Ears catch at curtains of fog, musing drizzles.
No pills can tranquilize to allay
America, our mother, whose daughter's
ransom price daily rises higher. No loan
will liberate her, wedded among the jesters,
and abandoned to the moneyed bankers.

Crooked Moon

Valentine's Day

The early morning moon shines crooked
light, near-half-eaten in February's
slow swallowing, that can still iridesce
the high cirrus. Dark, maybe-rain clouds
cannot erase, will wipe its clean face
clear again. It is light will blur its light,
a mightier to cast what had shone
steady—to show stumbling wanderers
a footpath when they should have been asleep—
into noon's oblivion. A sermon
stars do not speak of, that the morning
pen can only scribble, to copy Time's
writing in the skies, that repeats, fleeting,
repeats fleeting before unseeing eyes.

California Mornings

After the rains the mornings grow fat
again. Their shrubby cheeks glow pink
and red. Their green tresses fall long
and low. They scatter fragrance and wink
sun-beams extravagantly, careless,
feminine, and fickle, blowing cold and hot
both in one day. With names like April
and May, why should they fear the blot
of droughts ahead? Oh, the hours will be so
sweet. Sweet the blue and black berries
from farms watered by the March rains.
Sweet the peaches promised in the thickly
blossoming twigs. Sweet the vision of wine
decanted before sleep. Old memory
is dying as across the oceans
and beyond the mountains enemies
seem to dissolve with the sugar
in pies baking for California.
Fear is but the salt in their bread,
these young mornings in America,
rising, yawning to the pileated
woodpeckers' rat-a-tat-tat attacks
on bugs clustered in the bark of shade
trees, hidden vainly in the cracks.

In Praise of Limes

Come late March the limes appear on sidewalks
where we pick two, three, or five most mornings
for our breakfast table. Careless branches
drop sweet-sour green-yellow fruit, like flinging
gum to a crowd all through April and May,
until neighbors tire of plenty; excepting
the newcomers, for whom, decades passing,
plenty remains a miracle. Each day
unexpected, each morning miraculous
sunrise in a new country. Although *want-want*
blows like Santa Anas sparking ashes
on roof shingles, lounges and awnings,
under dry fronds above bungalows, although
coyote lairs in brittle eucalyptus
burn. Although in uneasy zigzag land
rifts, although thirst and desert brown
the homeless children of plenty,
although new and old split apart, unknown
to each other, we will persist in praising
the lime tree spring, newcomers to our town,
too many for the breaking earth to tear down.

The Incomplete Gardener

The incomplete gardener keeps tugging
her plot, tufts snagging soil: weeds, weeds.
She hasn't begun gardening although
it's been planned for years, she calculating
months, weeks, for spring rains, summer suns.
When the year's done, the Nursery's
never yet visited, tiny pots—
oregano, dill, sage and thyme, plants
sighed over, un-bought. Farmers markets' chilly
slowly dries, scarlet-tipped fruit,
root-bound in plastic container by
October. Immigrant from a country
with sunny rain, she's never mastered
seasons. Procrastination's the clock's
presentation when she remembers to check
time. It's late for zucchinis. Later
still for Big Boy seedlings. Too late for seeds
before next year's tufts spring up—weeds, weeds.

Serendipity

Just opening rose petals,
lavish lavender, drooping
fuchsias, lemon myrtle,
orange blossoms snowing
on ground, hidden baby pips:
color and green she hardly
understands trail and drip
scent in the bird-song eyrie.
Low geranium, high cypress—
potlatch of California—
like the two sleepers
huddled on bus bench, beer
bottles at feet, she feels
the addled air and reels.

April Heat Wave

Almost eighty degrees Fahrenheit
by nine a.m. Noon is dead still oven-
baked. Evening stays solstice bright.
Nature has run ahead to quicken

the months. The palms grow toothpick thin, bean
stalk tall, bracts withered feather dusters
against a blue burnt white. Seven years lean
predicting rain with sundowner blusters,

I've forgotten how not to hope. We throw open
the windows, draw water we do not have,
as if wishes are promises are heaven
on earth, and here and now forever safe.

Summer Camp

The sign says, "Parents:
Lost and Found." Do not
trust it. Parents are
so seldom found, so
easily lost. "What
are you doing next?"
a parent asks. "We're
doing nature," a child
says proudly. "Berries,
nuts, and seeds," the young
woman says, in combat
boots and dirty tee-shirt.

Farmers' Market

Beets, leeks, fennel, *kailan*. The vet,
self-proclaimed, in the wheelchair wasn't
at his corner the last two Saturdays—
that is, if he is who he says
he is.
           Hmong stall. How do I know
the farmers are from Fresno?
Isn't Fresno a ways from here?
Every Saturday all year
they offer Thai basil, scallions,
lemon grass, *bok choy*, onions
papery-skinned, just picked they say.

The vet, if he is who he says
he is, would be tall if he stood up.
Bone and skin, under the lap
cover layered over knees, no
begging sign. A simple can into
which we drop our weekly note.

If he isn't at the market,
I'd know he's passed. Not all gray-
headed, disheveled, wheel-chaired, gray-
bearded men are vets with no home.
Nor did all vets serve in Vietnam.

I am headed to the Hmong site.
Kangkung branches, *daikon* scrubbed white,
curved as calves of a well-fed woman.
                              Flash of Asia's wet-
markets in cool California,
my weekly nostalgia.

Garlic, fish sauce, soy stir-fry
to keep me unbound, walking: I
in the market, while the homeless vet,
if he was who I thought he was, yet
may be lying in a nursing home,
rusting knee hinges, withered ham.

Am I who I say I am? Are you?
There is enough guilt for those who
come with tides, ocean-borne, who are
born in the soil—all bound to America.

Monday Morning Road

(1969-2016)

Bottlebrush grown into tall trees make an avenue
of a suburban tract. I pick heavy Hass avocados
off a sidewalk, inveterate scrounging others' excesses
in a country's sidewalks, fruited like plains viewed
from a Greyhound through glassy flatness of green
stalks just before late-August tractors harvest corn
to feed the nation of tall sons headed off to 'Nam.
I'd fled, counter-wise, malarial jungle steam,
to find myself in killing snow. Now 'Nam is a story
another tall generation won't read, while I, emerged
out of winter's swaddling cloaks into Pacific sunshine,
count pennies again for perhaps another country
of ice and snow. No one escapes those jungle memories
grafted in the breaks straitened where the healing should be.

Shelter

Neither father nor mother followed
Eastwards to the West.
She did not think: bereft.
Did not figure: one, alone, single.
Strange bodies talked and schemed.
Strange avenues, skyscrapers, dangled
in nightmare and dream.

Orphaned in America, the strange
grows old, a family
of fidgeters, forgetters, arranged
mismatched roommates. The tree
of life wobbles, uprooted again
and again, lean crooked,
like the new country's lines, drawn in sand,
in blood and profit.

Here's the geography of souls who
will believe only
what they can see, will only view
what they can touch. Be
only where they are not. Shelter
is your name, new land.
Homes left behind, mother and father
buried, only the grand
story of spirit rescues even
as it shames our selfish heaven.

Tabula Rasa

Tabula rasa: the light from street lamps
when it's still dark before seven a.m.,
when the dark of rain on roads gleams.
Double urgent headlamps of the first bus
to town, bright windows empty of travelers,
except for a sole, slumped vacant, not viewing,
passing these street lamps left behind.
It is never *tabula rasa*. It says
to one, *You're home.* To the other,
Why are you approaching away?
Always away, the way weary, the way
Hopper saw the city you saw and see
all over America. No, not
tabula rasa: the first time the child
looked out of the homeless window
at a street lamp by a Malacca cross-road,
emak disappeared, *baba* disappeared,
hunger so close it no longer pressed,
in the first knowledge of loss: this knowing
what you will bear, stamped ineradicable.

Otherness

is all around us, at us: unremembered,
familiar. Entering the woods each day,
leaves, thorns and boles remain unnamed.
Outside, demanding ears, the highway's
eight-wheeled trailers, motor-homes utterly
other to our destination: Americans
at home in their Americanness, struck by
immigrants, like Earth comet-stricken,
averse to the universe outside. Like we
are various in ourselves, our bodies growing
estranged kin, members dangerous
to selves, this other common family,
Death; and even before, to be walking
someday and seeing only otherness:

Where am I? Where the way home? Who am I?

What Rough Beast?

It's me, Ruth,
slouching to
who knows where.
It's me—the
Palace grounds
are secured,
the woods fenced,
the houses
red-lined, seats
reserved, fruits
forbidden,
streets barred to
one walking.
Have you a
permit? Are
you licensed?
Your papers,
documents,
ID cards?
Speak, Ruth, when
spoken to,
only not
now, not here.

Illegitimi Non Carborundum

In the day's dispirited grinding round,
When praise reprises venom, and straight's bent,
Don't let the bastards get you (stay strong!) down.

There's one in every corner, every town,
Waiting for an error, a slip of pen
Forced by the daily workplace grinding round.

You lie low, out of the running, head down.
An ex-lover snarks with a best girlfriend:
That's who the bastards are who put you down.

When the big one rolls and the mortgaged ground
Breaks to the world's *schadenfreude*, oh then
Begins our every day's dispirited round.

Add devil winds, gusting sparks at sundown
Torching eucalyptus to furnace, again
The bastard fires will burn you down.

Now hate spills over fences, and its sound—
Expletive, silence—to invective lends
In this day's dispirited ugly round,
Do not—don't let its bastards grind you down.

Things That Make Me Happy

That I rise at 3 a.m. to write.
That everywhere is full of poems,
not just in America.

That I am reading Wislawa Szymborska.
That there are more of her poems
I have not read and will read.

That the women who gifted me
spite to keep their hate burning
are still alive to keep me warm.

That tomorrow is always a cliché,
a new page to be messed up, scrawled
with passing moments, and moments

can be stopped on a page to stand still.
That there are brothers to love, husband,
son, and strangers who reappear

to take on the name of family.
That there are worse times. That history
proves the worst we do to each other

will not destroy love for each other
in other times and other places.
That there is good coffee at breakfast

and good bread, and they will do for walking
in a city not yet destroyed.
That in the present drought and coming

great hatred there will be mornings when
you cannot sleep but will count syllables
beyond malice to a place like secure.

Hunter's Moon

October moon stays up late, bold
till seven a.m., long after
the wild night horses have been stabled.
She's mistress to the huntsman,
bare-breasted through the dark hours,
spot-lit queen of showgirls. Back East,
meaning Pacific West, where men
plough and sow and plant, she'd been
Mother, the one who'd built
the bridge for lovers crossing east
to west, west to east. An old woman
who's crossed that bridge, I watch
the huntsman, bold in the spotlight,
ride his dark horses out in daylight.

Vox Populi Vox Dei

"The voice of the people is the voice of God."

The voice bellowing from the stage
will not be upstaged. The rage
swelling from its undercurrents
is its own fixed swirling warrant

when actor and audience are one.
One, the agent and their actions.
One, litigant and ombudsman.
When the voice of God is human,

one is the voice of the people.
Scattered—the lame and the crippled,
when the voice of God is human
and bellows on stage from this man.

Cassandra

(November 8, 2016)

This Cassandra opens a bottle of red,
begins drinking early alone, in bed.

Fascism with a friendly face does not
console, his leers do not cheer, that knowing nod

to end times was foretold in the entrails
blasted by unreturned fire. They who were hailed

heroes in their homeland enter the temple,
swagger, swearing, seared in the Sun-King's call

to torch and burn. This Cassandra has no gift
for light. She's depressed. No Thanksgiving will lift

her day. No deeds already in the doing
can be undone. The blood in the sheetings

that she sees, the world that's winding down,
and none to scare, none can tell, none.

The Laws

Law of the stone:
I smash, I own.

Law of the flower:
Live for the hour.

Law of the bee:
No flight is free.

Law of the man:
I rule, I ban.

Law of the sun:
Above me, none.

Re-Reading *Moby Dick*

I.

The first twenty pages, and I am bored,
reading slowly like a ball-point pen
not quite dried that a push may not yet
leave a scratch still visibly alphabet.
That white whale monster hasn't appeared.
The schooner drives through ceaseless water,
blubber boiling in every vat, the fat
of oceans to tow to New Bedford.
The captain sails his ship still further.
Watch out sharp for the hulking white mass!
The mystery of crazed mastery that's
sent near mad near two centuries of scholars'
instinct for meaning—that giant white
fish forever eluding their white pages.

II.

I am weary after twenty pages,
already introduced to Ishmael
at parties and book fairs, each brave Ishmael
bonded to his captain, loquacious in mind,
looking out to make his fortune. He's
set up as American allegory,
American tragedy, epic of English
Only, oceanic consciousness
in floods of words.
                    Land calls. The lowly mint
colonizes. This is our un-legendary

present. Rain delays. Succulents deny
their name and live without water. Our
desert earth bears green spikes and bones
of immigrants bleached in the sun.

Oxymoron

Santa Barbara winter: an oxymoron
confusing with peonies, neon-lit. Beckons

excessive pink elegance. Stout trees,
orange globes almost as pushy

as silicone-injected boobs, and lemons
glimmering on green branches and thorns,

little sunrises. Only humanity's
covered her nakedness. She's

clothed in dark and bright, carapace
in steel and heart hurt, thoroughly surfaced,
oxymoronic, cabined to the last.

Grass

Like grass, the commonest cliché,
is love, trodden, yet everywhere,
whether sprung green or high stacked hay,
as grass, the commonest cliché,
we like cattle must bear away
its simple mouthfuls—everywhere
needful, grass, the commonest cliché
to love, trodden everywhere.

The Creek

The Maria Ygnacio Creek that runs
to the Pacific is dry again.
It is almost always dry, a sand bed
which skunks and possums, tails up, tread
along their way to backyard bins filled
with uneaten dinners, brown lettuce,
and squishy tomatoes that human hosts
don't bother to lid. Some edibles spill
daily, leftovers of our appetite.
We'd rather go hungry than eat someone's
throw-away dinner. Raccoons are not so
nice. Yesterdays' rains will not return.
Between yesterday and today, the rivulet
stays dry, our bins fill and overflow

No Rain Sonnet

To begin, the blank in the air early
morning, waiting as with the days before
for rain. The sequence shifts languidly,
as if pause is permanent, sough
of dry leaves nothing moving while we
eavesdrop with the kitchen clock for the hour
when water is to be welcomed, free,
the way it used to be. What hover
are mists that pale and lighten, fade and sink
into ocean. It will not rain today
nor tomorrow. Rain season is over
just as it's begun. Petals pink
before they brown. Sod toughens to clay.
Hades gravels cacti in chain-mail cover.

Saving

Even with drought, with grey greasy
water the wild grass grows,
shallow roots trolling in veiny
networks, to sprout yellow-
baby patches, and all in one
morning burst monstrous
straw filaments robust
as bushes in a rainy
fallow year.
             Even goats may
not eat it that gnaw on cacti thorn,
lip tires in abandoned canyons.
True trees need deep watering,
and there is none to be had today
when sunshine is a curse
and stark skies blush for nothing
at dusk and dawn. Shamelessness undoes
us—spigots flowing, saving
grey water for roots that alone
can trawl these withered earths.

At the Supermarket

I get into my car
and drive to the supermarket
at the edge of recorded heat
to stare at ice creams—sugar

and milk, silvery crystals all
the way from elsewhere, from slow
cows, hormone-pumped pregnant.
Shivering in the aisles (Fall

pre-set for the sun-stricken)
packed with people, everywhere
packed with us, reaching getting,
lining up rows on rows human,

quick to pride, mouth busy, face
wanting cool earth rare in a hot
planet, smiling at babies
welcomed to the human race.

Heat Waves

Ocean waves hello to new found sand.
Fronds, green as mermaids, wave strands
Goodbye, dried like kelp piled high on land.
Beach becomes water. Water turns to salt.
Wadis engulf to desert. Winters halt
Rains, Spring doesn't show up, and Summer bolts
His door. Heat decides to stay, waves away
All goodbyes, and dictates to Fate today,
                Everyday.

Wake!

Wake! Skies will blue in bleakest season.
Wake! Tipping on the horizon, the sun,
one, only, for eternity, if eternity
is, rises. Wake! December moves on,
a name that arbitrates nothing. The year
is ending. Or it begins. Leaves mass sodden
under barren wood, regularity
of time worn, underfoot, trodden. Trodden,
the walker who's slept through the century,
somnambulant as snails trailing tear
tracks over lemon groves. The promise
of returning light weakens. Nothing insists
forever. The cycle of summer and ice
stumbling shakes awake all of your paradise.

THE FIRE LAND

"HURRY UP PLEASE, IT'S TIME"
T.S. Eliot, "The Waste Land"

Evacuation

"The magic flute will protect you, and sustain you in the greatest misfortune."

—Emanuel Schikaneder

We sleep fully dressed, shoes
beside on the ready,
in the stream of history
waiting to flee, flute in hand.

Stillness is the door ajar,
cornucopia the flames
before it, magic that tamed
wildness less magic than quotidian.
No wildness waits to be tamed.
Fire is what burns. What burns

all that is weak, that is strong,
burns the rare and common.
Furies in the West bear, sudden,
the wild beast flute in their breasts.

Smoke

There's smoke in the air.
Los Angeles is burning.
Ventura has burnt.
Home in Asia
where smoke is smog is
dying, snorkelers
swim round paradise
islands that are drowning.
Poetry is sometimes
tragic, although not
like this, recording,
not imagining, times
when bleeding sunsets
snapped in pixels signify
fires to rage this year,
next year, through forever,
never to come, and smoke that's
in the air, everywhere.

Keepsakes

"Golden lads and girls all must as chimney sweepers come to dust." William Shakespeare

At 2 a.m. the squawking line
declares *emergency alert*, red flags
waving for Carpinteria, oh yet
distant, distant, to the south. We scour our bags
for the radio, battery-operated,
when flickering lights disappear,
the little promised-internet
box aluminum dull, not networking.

We fiddle with emergencies,
ignorant of how to, where to, when to
find the wherewithal, leave, run, drive,
knock on doors, beseeching. At five or so
the line squawks again its mandatory,
mandatory order: Montecito
up up up hup, before lights go
again, power-lines down, transformers
popping balloons at end of a party
someone—not us—had held after
everyone's asleep.
    And here in Goleta,
away from estates of old oak avenues,
cypress that shields mansions, we
of a different class look over the paltry
gathered, hard-gained, bargained for
in bazaars and markets, won in hunt or

love. Nothing's worth the keeping:
keepsakes a funny nervous giggle
in the dawn-dark where ashes spell
lessons still in the learning.

Santa Claus Lane

It begins to snow,
     silver sprinkles
     on chocolate cake hills
     of Santa Barbara.
Sweet California,
     fattening sweeter with each
     season,
it's snowing ash
     on your desserts
     Porsches
     your mice and men.

Massachusetts snows
     stay white   blinding   for
     an hour,
     a day
go grey
     with feet and cars.

Think of this
     white,
     blowing
     gently in from
Inferno
     to the South,
     bits of Aussie
     eucalyptus,

Russian
>	wild mustard,
>	fronds that waved for
>	Cleopatra.

Snow
>	with no crystal hexagon,
>	with sorrow
>	from a crematorium:

someone's
>	wedding memory,
>	forensic
>	clues from a bed

where lovers
>	thrashed or
>	a mother
>	sickened.

Ash
>	from ashes of a father
>	left on the mantel,
>	forgotten.

Flight up Highway
>	Thirty-three
>	to safety,
>	another county.

Crisp covered
>	tall trees
>	bud-less
>	three seasons

rainless,
      cars, cars, cars
      crowding
      driveways,
snow on their windows,
      waiting
blizzard.

The Fireman's Wife

Their child stays indoors,
purifier blowing
the house air clear
for his homecoming.
He'd put his ear
to her womb, the heart
of the unborn beating
goodbye at the door.
The winds elsewhere
are blowing, whistling
through the canyon
bearing torches before
them. Alarms beckon.
He'd trained for this part,
axe, hose, mask, yellow
uniform, amulet
round his slender neck, eyes
hooded like the owl's.
Such a man she'd wanted—
sweetly muscled,
such as the fire gods call
away in the sunrise.

Wolf Moon

Wolf moon bright lights black
sky, first night of January,
radiates through smoke.

California Skies

(The Holiday Fire, Goleta)

skies
    with no clouds
skies
    bleached by sun
skies
    heavy with winds
skies
    black in the hills
skies
    red in the blue
skies
    hissing in brush
skies
    crackling in branch
skies
    noisy with wings
skies
    dry with white rain
skies
    roofless, rueful—
        only
sky.

Sunrise In the West

Sunrise, a long glow in the West,
along the horizon ridge, false
daylight. The east turns a dim blue
filter. No one walks this poisonous
morning. Yesterday's ash drifts,
imperceptible kills.
Ashes of yesterdays past
cover groves, Santa Ynez hills,
birds of paradise, and roofs
no longer shelter where sparks fly
on Santa Ana winds. Like bodies'
worn mortality, the sun's a sickly
blotch in a grim sky, neither securing
when once we rose cleanly bright,
unchallenged. Draping elves and reindeer,
still shine the Christmas fairy lights,
ash-snow-covered, Target-points-earned,
beside where it's burning, has burnt, will burn.

This Frost

This frost does not melt, white
on blue tarp, white on red
bricks, white on half-ripened
oranges: the street is bright

dry sunshine, full empty,
cats and canines shut indoors.
No woodpecker drums, bores;
no humming bird, ruby-

headed, flits in purple sage
covered with hoarfrost;
no easy breathing on this lost
morning, particles on hedge

cutting a trench in chests. This
is frost no scraping can clear.
Wintery fig trees bear
branches stippled with ashes

that will not melt, shifting
suspended heavy metal
by heavy metal particle,
wind sifting, uplifting, grifting.

Fog After Fire

Fog in topmost eucalyptus branches
lingers longer, long after it's lifted
off pinyon and manzanita. Visitant
at the door, no morning sun reproaches,

urges farewell. The entire high atmosphere
bears moisture, cold blanket on a fevered
body—foliage stripped bare, not barren.
Pod, seed and nut, berry and shriveled

root, each spore, grain and budding ear
by the scorched trail, blackened, soot-edged,
green sprouts, every weed is welcomed. All praise
to the fecund, the newborn that suckle
purblind, germy and damp in the blasted
top soil, the corpse of their winter mother.

WILD LIFE

The Wind

The wind is soughing
                and sighing
in the branches, rifling
their myriad leaves
               for havoc.
Winter is over.
            The young leaves frolic
and will not fall.
            I'm sad, I'm sad,
she says. *No branch will break, no leaf add*
to the dead although
I blow and I blow.
But here comes a woman walking.
                  I'll

whip her hair and chill
her cheeks and see how she bends
to my heavy hand.
And like the trees
the woman gladly
           lends her ears to the sighing air,
although her head's uncovered, and she
herself is bare, bare, bare.

Ladybird

On my wrist, orange black-pepper-spotted wings:
a bright mole on unnourished bone
incapable of thickening
after childhood's starvation. I whisper,
Fly away home. It doesn't listen,
crawls on skin taut through five times seven
years of plenty—as if food were a mirage,
crammed larder and cans past used-by date
scant security reckoned against reckless
countries. The wee creature doesn't reckon home,
will not fly away, its smidgen beauty resting
minutes on bare, near-barren flesh that twitches
under its weight; then rises on a second
whisper, into nest-less sunshine, unfixed, home.

Gopher Stones

Some mornings I'm minded to pick
stones from the middens the gophers
have thrown up, invisible gophers
whose busy cities make holes
out of gardens and lawns. Whole
hosts of them live with us right in
our quiet streets where fences
and fancy front doors stand between
burglar and home. I bend for
the smooth pebbles lying in dirt,
mud-brown, warm as fruit in June.
Neighbors lay tarp, chicken-coop wiring
against these intruders like they've
set alarms and motion sensors
to fend off the larger dangers.
Walking, I'm filling my pockets
with stones. The gophers unearth new
ones each morning, the unsealed
ground pocked with gaps for breathing
in burrows where we'd keep them,
unseen, the way we are living,
surface-bound in our houses—
countries below, four walls above.
I carry the stones they throw out,
pocketful by pocketful, plant
them, unwashed, in garden pots
so over-watering will not rot
the sweet roots of herbs and flowers,

saving, as always, what's worthless.
We who love rocks bless the ground
that grows them, grit and gravel,
boulder or gem, that have worked free
out of fiery cauldrons, rising
millennia on millennia
from a core ceaselessly molten,
to knock on our shins, infuriate
farmers: to teach to love hardness,
the cold stony-hearted flung
so far from their centers only gophers
will move them, hard pebbly
signs that someone's still breathing
below, sunk deep in the tunnels.

Social Distancing

The Monarchs seem not to have heard
of Covid-19, I think this April,
the few appearing in our backyard
sentient non-Sapiens in the navel
orange branches. We only seem alike,
liberated by sun. Locked down, we envy
their brief spring flirting with the garden shrike
among white blossoms posed like bridesmaids' posies.
For us, knowledge of good and evil
weigh down, weight turning to adipose
tissue with each generation still
taller, thickening. Even the thin are obese
next to these Monarchs in their airwaves
unweighted by knowledge of extinction.
Wingspans smaller than when gold-black air
first flashed me, they keep social distance to stave
off heavy-bellied Sapiens, distance that bears
both lardy lolling and variegation.

Owl Says

Owl says at midnight:
Give away everything
So you can get what you want.

Owl says at daybreak:
If you have nothing
You have nothing.

Wild Life

Field mouse in your wee house,
hidden from glare of sun and stare
of poison spray, Burns loved you,
as we do not, your sooty
trembling tail scaring the fine
ladies of Santa Barbara.
You do not dare the open day
though fat seeds tempt. Your whiskers
shiver at each deafening
footfall. The lives above—below,
your cramped barrow!—are running wild,
wide and broad and tall, while
their nice ladies shriek at your
disappearing shadow.

Lizards Are Us

The lizards are out, multiple tails
unfurled, July sun beckoning
to the sizzling sidewalks hot enough
to cook a bunch of eggs, easy-side up,
bellies basking in summer surrender:
summer people crawling out of shelters,
hidden from tabbies who'd tear their heads off
sooner than they'd lick their orange-furred
undersides. Darwin knew Nature's
incentive that had his spirits sunk.

Adapt! Stay locked indoors! Your hot blood
broils here where others sun
away from wringing tails. Quietus, evolving
rapid extinction, rises above beetled-trunk
and roof, above lizards in purple-spray
undergrowth—rising, the easy way
friendship is survival, lacking
combat conviction, choosing to fail
with the cold-blooded in the closing day.

Bees

Everyone's graying
except everyone who's
stirring the bees
in their hollows.
I do not envy
lovers lying
under trees
barbed by kisses
of innumerable stings.

Squawk

Crow squawks above me in the day,
an echo of calls that wake at
2 and 4, before sun with soft touch
rouses, and although I turn away
from these alarms, just as I
walk away from its interruption
of my solitary silence, its call,
that abrupt challenge in the sky,
echoes in the pacific morning
its pitched single-note blare
to shake off the mind's harmony
humming over the wretched breaking
of the earth, that will not scare
but sound, resound, squawking, ugly.

Firefly

Something wakes me up on Saturday night. A firefly is winking its 1 a.m. code in my bedroom. Insomniacs, we both watch the cold response of the VCR time-dial, its green glow winking a newer code. The firefly whizzing in the pitch-black space flashes like a semaphore. I know its instinct working here. The bug cannot help itself, deluded by the high-tech clock, timing its luminescent rhythms to an ancient sense, as I had done in my firefly days, and now acknowledge another urgent flashing in the encroaching blackness, signaling for another kind of light, deluded like the zany bug bumbling between the closet and the faux Georgian bureau. Or raise to thought the insight of correspondence as Dante would have it, divine illumination. Or foolish as an unthinking insect unrecognizing correspondence, only an unmarked likeness unworthy of meaning, of carnal deed, of divine desire. Those rhythms that pullulated at twenty swell my head at thrice that age. Growing old says nothing about older creeds, although it may make a former act and later thought collaborate, betraying the common sense of reason that mocks the firefly in its courting of a VCR electric clock. So, I cogitate on the sum of being and life which swarm phosphorescence outside the summer screens.

Prayer For Coyote

Snatching fast fleeing bunnies,
digging at shallow mole-holes,
licking the dew-brushed bayberry
branches when the creek bed molts
into shattered baked clay ruts:
mistress of opportunity,
her whelps' unceasing whimper cuts
her, and she must dare where she
cannot go—under the fence through
damp colored ground. Ancestress,
teach her to live when her dugs, milk-less,
hang low; to pad, jaw and sinew
strung, an old cat caught in the daisies,
across the creek, back to her babies.

Alarm

Clock, beeping, pitched
to reach the street
where I walk, pitch
dark, head and feet
paying mind to
the uneven
pavement. Who
is awakened
and from what dreams?
The alarm sounds,
insistent, streams
across the ground
I cover—birds,
sleepers, and I
caught in its absurd
continuous cry.

Praise Song for the Pause

Praise the morning fog
drying in the morning sun.
Praise the dry April streets'
absence of puddles.
Praise absence, the hustling
streets' busy absent.
Praise the busy, the loud birds'
chittering play, hidden in leaves.
Praise the quiet snails, horns
hidden, persistent on adobe.
Praise the persisting outdoors'
feral cats and coyotes.
Praise the feral world,
suddenly unafraid.

Shadow Of Monarchs

Shadows of Monarchs
On the woods-shadow-speckled
Sun-winding trail home.

Saving My Own Skin

"If I am not for myself, who will be?
If I am only for myself, what am I?
If not now, when?"
                                    Rabbi Hillel

"The coronavirus is here in New York, here now."
                                    Governor Andrew Cuomo

It is here in Wuhan, in Hubei, here now.

It is here in Hong Kong, here now.

It is here in Taiwan, here now.

It is here in Singapore, here now.

It is here in South Korea, here now.

It is here in Italy, here now.

It is here in Iran, here now.

It is here in Spain, here now.

It is here in France, here now.

It is here in Germany, here now.

It is here in Austria, here now.

It is here in Australia, here now.

It is here in the United Kingdom, here now.

It is here in Thailand, here now.

It is here in Vietnam, here now.

It is here in Turkey, here now.

It is here in Canada, here now.

It is here in the United States, here now.

It is here in Japan, here now,

It is here in Malaysia, here now.

It is here in India, here now.

It is here in Brazil, here now.
It is here in Ecuador, here now.
It is here in South Africa, here now.
It is here in Zimbabwe, here now.
It is here in Russia, here now.
It is everywhere, here now.
Saving my own skin, here now.
What am I, here now?

Morning Panic

The Eastern gray squirrel,
immigrant like me, scampers
yards ahead, panicked by this
solitary mammal who ambles,
masked obscured as the peanut-
sharing pal, to huddle under
a car, one of many stranded
curbside, unpolished. What
lies ahead for us, domestic
and wild, panicked this morning
by sudden appearance? I—
by children springing frantic
outdoors, escaping mother,
virus-bearing humans—scuttling
to hide in a house, one of many
scrubbed homes lined like neighbors,
street after street emptied, town
after town ghosted, locked down.

Ode to Covid-19

Too little too late was not the white
evening jasmine on time late March
profligate over the tall fence,
shutting private locked-downs from
Main Street America.
                       They'll fall
through the weeks, the last fragrance
brown grit on stepping stones,
                     so many
just in time making way for Easter
lilies blooming in the grass below climbers.
Never *unchartered waters, challenges
unprecedented.*
                  Every spring
springs unprecedented. In nature
the normal is always unprecedented
ever the new normal.
                  The aged mortal
is the normal
                     rage against the dying.
Moral resignation
                     resigned to the dying
of light in the sun's western fury,
streets emptied, darkening with night
as was from the Beginning,
                    Wordless,
agape at the speed Death leaps,
                     human

to human to human. Before this power
how small we are/I am under
the pan-shadow of this tiniest

                          viral speck.

Eucalyptus Country

Wind in the eucalyptus shushes,
wheezes loudly, no one under branches.
Widow-makers, I was warned, so many
made so when, cracking like canons, leafy
canopies' graceful draperies break heads,
crush cyclists and cars. I walk in dread,
in love with Nature each spring. Stingy rains
run out. Eucalyptus' languid skeins
tan brown and browner than beach bathers
pickled in UV rays June to September.
This May's early sundowners prepare
for fire season when eucalyptus flare
like matchstick bunches lighting California.
For now, we welcome this evening air
stirring through every sunburnt unbuilt ground,
virus cleared—between plague and fire, locked down—
between distant neighbors, all seeming null,
waiting our human-cleared autumnal.

Heron

The gray blue heron slowly stalks
the mown grass-flats of the hilly
park. I have sighted them in years
of early solitary walks,
each viewing a breath-indrawing,
like a first sun sighting in the east,
Akhenaten reborn each dawn.
I fumble for the image, shuttering
the camera in my chest, its click
too distant to scare the hungry
elegant gent off the gophers
airing in dew-moist puddles thick
with roots. Time shutters my image,
prey in its marshes, my wild life caged.

Akin

"We are all in this together"
Antonio Guterres

In the pandemic
the meanest flower is akin to me,
who's akin to a hundred thousand and growing neighbors,
who're akin to three hundred and fifty thousand and growing
    extended family,
who're akin to six and a half billion distant cousins,
who're akin to billions of passenger pigeons,
who were akin to uncountable trilobites that sank into the
    Paleozoic waters,
from where the first web-footed fish crawled out,
akin to reptiles preying on the small warm-blooded,
who're akin to mammals suckling their just-born,
who're akin to me,
akin to the meanest flower.

What Comes After?

What comes after the chrysalis?
Perhaps sun and flight.
What comes after the butterfly?
Perhaps darkened light.
What comes after the mourning dove?
Perhaps perfect quiet.
What comes after lonely silence?
Perhaps new delight.
What comes after white spring blossom?
Perhaps purple plum.
What comes after years and losses?
Perhaps parts and sum.
What comes after a question asked?
Perhaps wisdom.

AFTERWORD

AFTERWORD

By Boey Kim Cheng

TWO walks, two coasts. First, on our left the glittering estuarial end of the Hunter River decanting into the sea as we head towards the headland, on which sits the round tower of Nobbys Lighthouse, gleaming white in the morning sun. Home for the poet is beyond the horizon on the other coast of the Pacific, but she seems at home here in the antipodean coastal landscape, her keen eyes revelling in blue expanses of water and sky, her determined stride keeping her willowy frame on an even keel in the cold blasts sweeping in along with the crashing waves. Flash forward a decade, and I am keeping pace with her on a headland overlooking the white stucco spread of Santa Barbara landward, and the slate grey of the Pacific on our left. If there is a constant in the restless, questing poetry of Shirley Geok-lin Lim, it is the coastal landscape, especially the Pacific littoral of Santa Barbara, a habitat and ecosystem that has sustained much of her work as a poet and scholar.

In "Past Danger and Drowning," inspired by the Newcastle coastline, Lim sings a paean to the Pacific, calling her muse "the ocean woman" and describing her morning walk to the beach thus: "Mornings I set off for the Pacific,/ Her heaving bosom stretched between/ Rivals gazing from opposite shores" ("Past Danger and Drowning," *Walking Backwards*). In an elegy for her father staged on a Santa Barbara beach, she negotiates her way between past and present, between places and lives through the liminal coastal space: "So now I look/ Out at the Pacific waiting for him/ To wash ashore here where I walk…" ("Cremation at Sea," *Listening to the Singer*). Between two coasts, two lives, Lim's poetry finds its meaning and inspiration and the vehicle for reconciling the two extreme reaches of her life. And the vehicle for discovering the submarine ties between them is the motif of crossing, which has underpinned her work since her debut 1980 Commonwealth Prize winner *Crossing the Peninsula*. Crossings and re-crossings have enabled her to map the in-between liminal space and render it fertile ground for poetic and scholarly work, the Trans-Pacific perspective affording an imaginative distance from which to see herself, her adopted home (Santa Barbara), her place of birth (Malacca), the past and present.

But while Trans-Pacific crossings, real and imaginary, yield the creative tension that drives her work, it can also breed a sense of transit, and exacerbate the sense of exile and displacement, with its attendant questioning of home and belonging. The migrant's loss of home and the sense of the fragility of habitat, which has long been a diasporic theme that runs through Lim's previous collections of poetry and works of fiction, is now translated in *In Praise of Limes* into an acute awareness of the vulnerability of the natural environment, and an attentiveness to flora and fauna of the Californian coast around Santa Barbara, which flags a significant spatial shift in Lim's oeuvre. Where her early collections gravitate towards Asia and her place of birth, and the middle-period work negotiates a balance between Asia and America, this new work is almost exclusively located on the eastern side of Pacific, more exactly in and around the Santa Barbara suburb where Lim has made a home. Where earlier poems inhabit predominantly urban and cosmopolitan spaces, forging Trans-Pacific, transnational links between east and west, the poems here are content with the parochial, with exploring the particulars of the local habitat, and discovering the balance between the human and the natural realms.

The poems here are firmly grounded in the Californian earth in a way that Lim's previous works are not, unsettled as they are by a sense of displacement and the pull towards Asia. *In Praise of Limes* is testament of the hard-earned love of the migrant for her adopted home. These are poems of homecoming, and of the pledge of love for the drought and fire-stricken country, a love that becomes stronger even as the threat of loss of home escalates. In previous collections Lim mourned the home that was forfeited with the act of migration and the dominant key was elegiac; here the potential destruction due to drought and fire has kindled a poetry of praise. The title, with its nod to Auden's "In Praise of Limestone," establishes the register of celebration that unifies the collection. There is gladness in the bountiful presence of these eponymous late-arriving fruit, "newcomers to our town/ too many for the breaking earth to tear down." In "The Incomplete Gardener" the poet is cultivating her plot with "oregano, dill, sage and thyme" and "calculating/ months, weeks, for spring rains, summer suns." She is reminded of the fact that as an "Immigrant from a country/ with sunny rain, she's never mastered/ seasons." But gardening is a means of settlement, allowing the migrant to grow a sense of belonging, as she attunes to the seasons, to the land's cycle of growth, death and regeneration.

The collection travels beyond the bounds of the poet's suburban home and garden to the "Eucalyptus Country," picking out the heron, ladybird, coyote, monarch butterfly, pinyon, manzanita, the eucalyptus, Australian trees that have gone native on California soil, and a medley of other wildlife and flora for praise. In a sense, the communion with nature is Covid-enforced, since the pandemic has curbed global travel which was vital to Lim's pre-pandemic work. "Akin" acknowledges this, with its echo of Wordsworth's lines, "the meanest flower that blows can give/ Thoughts that do often lie too deep for tears":

> In the pandemic
> the meanest flower is akin to me,
> who's akin to a hundred thousand and growing neighbors
> who're akin to three hundred and fifty thousand and growing
>   extended family
> who're akin to six and a half billion distant cousins,
> who're akin to billions of passenger pigeons…

The book's itinerary transcends the Trans-Pacific routes of Lim's previous works to glimpse something akin to a pantheistic, ecopoetic vision that transcends geopolitical boundaries.

The interconnectedness of life and the beauty of the natural world are however, under threat, and that danger is palpable in the central section of the collection "The Fire Land," as it tracks the season of "bleeding sunsets," "false daylight" and "snowing ash." The fires wreak destruction but also bring renewal, and a new cycle of regeneration and growth: "All praise/ to the fecund, the newborn that suckle/ purblind, germy and damp in the blasted/ top soil, the corpse of their winter mother." In earlier poems, Lim drew creativity from travel, from a sense of dwelling and moving between borders; here a sense of rootedness and the land and seasons feed the poet's thirst, the natural cycle providing an analogue for the creative process, as the poet, like the land, waits for the drought to break. Rain, the counterpoint to fire, is the most recurrent word in the collection, and its arrival brings much-needed relief and long-awaited release of creative energies: "Poetry/ needs rain in drought years like creeks/ need rain to murmur, like dried sticks/ need rain to root". The Eliotian imagery and elemental binary are reconciled in the soil, in the burnt earth stirring to life under the touch of rain.

The German poet Hölderlin says: "Wherein lies the danger, grow also the saving power." In Lim's previous collections, the echoes of a vanished or lost home are audible in poems that are obsessed with movement, betraying an anxiety about space and place. Here in *In Praise of Limes*, even as the threat of loss of home and habitat is heightened with the prolonged drought and encroaching fires, the poet's sense of where and what home is becomes stronger, clearer. It feels as though the question of home which Lim's work has pursued over the years in relentless Trans-Pacific movements between coasts, between worlds, has finally found some resolution, if not an answer.

Boey Kim Cheng is the author of *Between Stations, Gull Between Heaven and Earth*, and six poetry collections.

Acknowledgement is made to the following, in which some of the poems in this collection were originally published, some in slightly different form: "Passing Through," *The Irreversible Sun*, West End Press, 2015; "Otherness," *Anglistica*, Vol. 22, No. 1, 2016; "*Illegitimi non carborundum*: Don't Let the Bastards," *Nasty Women Poets*, Lost Horse Press, 2017; "Cassandra Days," "What Rough Beast?" "The Laws," *Feminist Studies*, 2018; "Evacuation," "Waiting for Santa Claus," *California Quarterly*, Vol. 44:1, 2018; "Saving," *Manoa*, 2019; "Wake!" "Santa Barbara Rain," "Spring Mornings," "What Comes After," "Winter Moon," *Journal of Transnational American Studies*, 2019; "The Wind," "Fog after Fire," *The Hudson Review*, 2019; "Shelter," "Ode to Covid-19," "Akin," *This is How We Come Back Stronger: Feminist Writers on Turning Crises into Change*, Feminist Book Society, New York: Feminist Press, 4/6, 2021; "Praise Song for the Pause," "What Comes After," "At the Supermarket," *International Journal of Pacific Asia Studies*, 2021; "Prayer for Coyote," "California Skies," "Social Distancing," *While You Wait*, Gunpowder Press, 2021.

I thank Dana Gioia for his Preface, Kim Cheng Boey for his Afterword, Emily Grosholz and R.S. Gwynn for their generous comments, Chryss Yost for her invaluable editorial eye, Miao Nie for the author's photograph, and Gwen Frankfeldt for front cover design. I am grateful to Shelley Fisher Fishkin, Nina Morgan, my family—Charles Bazerman and Gershom K. Bazerman—, Can Askoy, Vincenzo Bavaro, Kai Hang Cheang, Grace Chin, Dean Gui, Weihsin Gui, Tammy Ho, Joshua Ip, Klaudia Lee, Edwin Malachi, Eric Martinsen, Chingyen Mayer, Jason Polley, Angelia Poon, Shivani Sivagurunathan, Stephen Sohn, Tee Kim Tong, Gina Valentino, Nicoleta Alexoae Zagni, and many others for their encouragement.

ABOUT THE AUTHOR

Shirley Geok-lin Lim received the British Commonwealth Poetry Prize for *Crossing the Peninsula*, making her the first woman and first Asian to receive the prize. She has published ten poetry collections, most recently *The Irreversible Sun, Ars Poetica for the Day*, and *Do You Live In?* She has also published three chapbooks. Her poetry has been widely anthologized and published in journals like *The Hudson Review, Feminist Studies* and *Virginia Quarterly Review*. Her poems have been featured on television by Bill Moyers, on podcasts such as Tracey K. Smith's *Slowdown*, and set to music as libretto for various scores. She received American Book Awards for her edited anthology, *The Forbidden Stitch*, and her memoir, *Among the White Moon Faces*. She has been honored with MELUS and Feminist Press Lifetime Achievement Awards and UCSB's Research Lecturer Award. She is also author of three novels, *The Shirley Lim Collection*, three short story collections, and two critical studies, as well as editing or co-editing well over a dozen anthologies and special issues of journals.